Among the Trees

POEMS AND PHOTOGRAPHS

Cullen Whisenhunt

Fine Dog Press

AMONG THE TREES

Table of Contents

Image: Scissortailed Flycatcher (*Tyrannus forficatus*) in flight, Calera, OK, 2020

What I Hope We Remember

In this new normal, where
we're living life through peepholes,
peeking out from lonely bubbles
built to keep each other safe,

It is still good to venture out,
to take a walk or drive, remind
ourselves the sun still shines,
grass still greens, sky still blues.

That clouds still cling together
like Jack's mystic mountains,
and his treetop dancers still twist
and twirl lyrical, happy.

That now is still the season for scissortails,
sweeping in with the break of spring,
coming to rest on rusted fence line
and fanning famous tail feathers.

That redbuds still bloom, while
dogwood and pear tree petals
paint parks and parking lots alike
like shifting white-sand beaches.

And that road signs waist-deep in wildflowers
can still be just as welcoming,
and the wind can still wipe worry-sweat
from a fear-fevered brow.

March 2020

Visions of Durant, Oklahoma

> *who loned it through the streets in Idaho seeking visionary indian angels*
> *who were visionary indian angels*

—Allen Ginsberg, "Howl"

I saw him today, Allen.

Saw him as I blew
down Enterprise Boulevard
like an eastern wind.
Saw him framed above
the road in the unbroken
but backlit clouds.
Saw him in ragged blue jeans,
work boots, neon green
construction tee shirt, and smudge
of white helmet with
Choctaw Nation stamp.

Saw him with two great crane necks
rising up behind, sprouting
from his back like wing
spine mast poles waiting
to unfurl, pressing
the sky higher and higher
on hydraulic pistons,
freeing us to breathe and fly
and stoop no more.
Saw him like a new Coyote
trickster god, polycultural,
polyperson, vertex
of tribe and industry, holding
cedar sapling with one palm

and backhoe at bay
with another.
Saw him like titan Atlas,
with raw shoulders standing tall
on muddy mountain spine of Mother Earth.

Saw him later, hopscotching
railroad ties, just this side
of Arkansas in bleak light,
trafficky, kicking gravel
in flip-flops in dead winter,
Saw him with gothic trees
snaking up behind
to screen silhouette
of smokestack steeple.
Saw him with cigarette, puff-puffing
like the engine he watched screech
away, wondered what
he wondered while he wandered,
he in undershirt and sweats,
with mustache penciled,
too dark to mark his complexion.

Saw him on 7th, too, on
asphalt parking lot,
dancing in technicolor
costumes to Spanish music.
Saw him as many
children, circling up, holding hands,
dancing, singing, rehearsing.

Saw the both of him
hugging, being hugged
out on the front porch,
twisting high on Conversed toes,

blue jeaned and sweatered,
star-ankled and starry-eyed
behind glasses over a shoulder
and around the dark
hood of a brother,
prodigal perhaps,
or always there and loved
just the same.

Saw her squeeze
her smile into his
chest, under long hair,
peeking at the road, at who
might be watching, daring them,
daring all of us,
to say or to love
anything this much,
this sure, this certain.

I saw him, Allen,
saw the visionary indian
angel that you sought.
I saw him, and he was everything
you never promised
and nothing more,
        But nothing less, too.

on the fringes of a fair
for Keely, after Lawrence Ferlinghetti

Had enough of Tulsa's Golden Driller
        Guthrie Green
        Gathering Place?

        Check out Utica
with its bunch'a churches 'bout to fall down
on top of bright black and yellow metal wheel-spoked
        yard art tanka inspirations,
or see the prestige of Yale besmirched
by derelict meat shoppe with bull mural broadside
        missing a shoulder for the sake of a window
and advertising "exotic" cuts out of everything
        from deer
to kangaroo.

Further on, find a golf ball warehouse all tin-walled
and muddy across from Mr Taco's
"there ain't no way in hell you'll finish this big-ass burrito"
        drive-through,
        backroad Oklahoma Place
for handmade fence toppers in animal
        monster humanoid shapes with secret interior carvings,
        and watch the wind talk rainbow pinwheels
        into buffering oblivion.

        Then slip through Gilcrease spotting
ugly-ass ducks out front of the School of Art,
colonial brick house gone full rainforest
        with shoots of giant green leaf
        and blue glass water bottles
        perched on every other fence spine

or sky-facing tree limb,
and a middle-aged man in short shorts
        and thin orange t shirt walking
        head on into cool straight-line breeze that shudders
        the yellow antifreeze jug swung left-handed.

Finally, ride the loop around downtown to eye pink Sky Blue Delivery
        trucks, the smiling Eskimo shouldering the brunt of American
        Cool, and a huge pair-of-pliers-looking pedestrian bridge
before heading out of town towards whatever
Mounds
        you came from.

Red Earth Redress

Oklahoma
Okla humma
"Red people"
Rednecks
      hillbillies, pig farmers, cattle ranchers,
      hay haulers, deer hunters, gun toters
Red-headed, red-handed, red-eyed
      dope smokers, crack dealers, and meth cookers
Bad Breakers
Broken promises in the Promised Land
Canaanites proudly wearing the buckle of the Bible Belt
      in God's country
FUCK Texas
"Red River rivals"
Crimson and cream smokes burnt orange any day
Boomer Sooner, Boomer Sooner
      Boomer Sooner Schooners sailed red dirt oceans
      and weighed anchor at boondocks
Where Deliverance descendants set up shop with banjos
      and shotgun weddings and Confederate flags
      and dead Indians and capitalist blood money
      and became religiously racist, radical, right-wing, Republicans
I mean, red state, right?

Wrong
    ...ish

Sure, Tulsa's arts district has tried to whitewash
      over the good ole days when oil barons,
      barrel racing, and race riots were all the rage,
When brown faces turned black and blue and the violet
      night sky was splashed red-orange by burning black gold.
And yes, some blue law believers are still fighting rainbows

and pink triangles while their own hometowns
    are so far in the red that no amount of blood money
    can keep greengrocers from blacking out windows.
But, down on the Red River, dead Indians now paint
    with all the colors of the windfall at Windstar and Choctaw,
Where greens, silvers, and coppers return to them
    straight from the pink and purple purses of blue-haired white ladi
Up in the city, black jazz and blues roots show that invisible men
    can at least leave musical footprints,
And of course, if you listen closely, these Oklahoma hills
    still echo Woody Guthrie lyrics about blue collar worker's rights
    and damn near Red Machine Communism.
In fact, just look skyward, and at the hills and valleys,
    at the plains and creeks and soil and bedrock,
And you'll see there's no state bluer, greener, or more golden,
    and all of it growing out of red, white, and black.

University Boulevard

Drive by and look at
stately, self-important windows,
sterile symmetry,
stratified, red-brick walls.
Watch as it exhales
people from within, leaving
leafy sidewalks, lawns
sloping to and from,
with waxy green tree and grass
blades and maybe blooms
blossom over, underneath
red-peeling benches.
Brilliant, illuminating
orbs where needed to
light ways to outside,
find spaces out and way out,
diasporic in daylight,
at night become
penultimate penumbra
parking lots and lots
of long walk, loneliness cars
on the outer curb.
Keep going, outside, outside,
now (be serious)
now, look left, to Spanish church
where workers, prostrate,
rest like the dead from rooftop
maintenance above
blue-stained glass images of
your god (their god also,
just a different tint).

Meditation

The leather magnolia
petals fall hard
as if to crack
the sidewalk, then lie
bowl-still beside
waxy leaves
already yellowed
by spring downshifting
into summer.

They twitch and skitter
like the bottlebrush tail
of a nearby red squirrel,
lifted by the slightest
breeze to be thrown
a-ground anew. But

the petals hold,
brown in the sun,
and wait to catch
a rain that will make
all things green
once more.

Meandering

Apparently, the whole world woke
to my word-of-the-day
calendar.

Couples,
arms linked, loll
out and away
from snowed-under
footpaths, reveling
in newfound freedom.

Cardinals, vivid
against the white
backdrop, short-hop
first one way,
then the other,
like flames.

And, of course, the flakes
themselves, causing all this
mess, float down without
any clear purpose,
ride this breeze, bounce
off that branch,

then alight, softly, on my shoes,
mid-shuffle.

Among the Trees

This, a mighty red cedar
in a crease between two hills
grows large, green, bristling
against wind, rain, all elements
and erosions. It is solid,
everlasting. It
barely sways.

But when the lowest boughs
are penetrated, they reveal
not a single tree, but a copse
of cedars grown so close,
so intimate,
their branches strip each other vulnerable.

Each trunk creaks
in the breeze, leans
one into another.
The storm outside
can do no more
than swish an exterior
twig or two, for roots
run deep wrap tight,
strong as anchors holding
the whole world down.

Image: Red Cedar (*Juniperus virginiana*) berries,
Ardmore Regional Park, Ardmore, OK, 2019

Statuary Sequence

for Keely Record

four-foot flamingo
rusting at the seams
dances with nature
beside butterflies
big as barn owls

        cement cat in spring garden—
        always sad

two concrete children,
arms crossed, tilted
into the same tree, counting
an eternal game
of hide-and-seek

        stone squirrel
        with prayer-clasped paws—
        above, acorns ripen

angels, saints, the virgin
Mary, and Jesus himself
with backs turned, casting
the first shadows—
long, deep, dark

Scattered Haiku

The morning after—
a cardinal alights
on burnt birch limb

Mid-winter—
birdsong softens lifeless limbs

The last days of spring—
cottonwood snowdrifts
swept away by warming breeze

Buzzard circles
over city cemetery
—seems redundant

Image: Northern Cardinal (*Cardinalis cardinalis*) in brambles,
Waterloo Park, Denison, TX, 2019

Bird Watching

A kidney bean of crows
floats over a crumbling
schoolhouse, stops
suddenly, elongates up
-wards like an arm made
entirely of freckles, stretch
-ing for attention. A bubble
of oblivious pinches off like
meiosis and blows on south
unnoticing.

Later, a decapitated vulture
carcass, rolled by a semi tire,
one elbow pinioned beneath,
wings a feathered acknowledge
-ment in my direction, its down
still wet with blood. I slide my car
just right and do not even think
to wave back.

Lampyridae

for Nana

A shadow floating behind headlights
lifts an evening cigarette and
drags once, flaring amber as it passes.

In the wake of you, I
imagine this the raising of a lone-ember salute,
the dripping ash an expansion of your urn,
the curling smoke the ascension of your soul.

I drift, as one does, past
the cemetery, where fireflies wink
back and forth over the tombstones
in short gasps, pulling pitiful,
perpetual attempts at lighting.

Raccoon Eyes

"Raccoon Eyes" he called the tree,
a red cedar with knotted sockets,
already old when they first moved in.
And he and Dottie laughed
at it together—at it
and at their dinner, at peaches and greens
from their garden of unlabeled
wedding pounding prank cans.
		And it watched them laugh and smiled.

Even then, it leaned,
heavy, on its neighbor,
the wild chinaberry.

And it grew and watched them plant
and grow new trees and gardens
and eventually children
right up out of the pasture.
Two boys, who laughed
at Raccoon Eyes just like
their daddy did, and who
climbed as high as Raccoon Eyes could go.
		And it watched them laugh and smiled.

And they could because it leaned,
heavy, on its neighbor,
the wild chinaberry.

And it grew and watched those boys
become men and those parents
grandparents, watched Terry and Dot
become Papaw and Memaw,
one telling jokes and the other
reading books to grandkids who grew
to know laughter and learning
and how to climb trees.
Who would laugh as they crawled
up Raccoon Eyes' sides.
          And it watched them laugh and smiled.

And they'd sit there while it leaned,
heavy, on its neighbor,
the wild chinaberry.

And it grew and watched her wilt,
Dottie, Mom, MeMaw,
under IV bags, bandanas, stethoscopes.
It watched her keep laughing,
and him keep laughing,
and them keep laughing, until
all the laughing stopped.

But then they started leaning,
heavy, on their neighbors.
          And it watched them lean and smiled.

Now, it survives alongside
new grandchildren, step-grandchildren,
young, laughing, grandchildren

who keep climbing, learning,
and it keeps watching
him, Terry, Papaw,
as he withers with a smile,
still laughing all the way down
onto the walker,
into the wheelchair.
        And watching him laugh, it smiles.

And they lean, heavy,
on each other, as neighbors,
Papaw Terry and
Raccoon Eyes.

In Morning

8 a.m. and the birds
are out in concert krilling
until the blonde pup
bounds up barking, matchsticks
mass migration from meadowlark,
quail-quick and quiet
underneath straight-line
blue jay and finch wing wind.

Only the redbreast remains,
perched on barbwire
or trusting enough to wait
in low branches
for the opportune time
to bounce away through nothing
but air—whole, free.

Revision, June 27

Night drops on this town
like dirt at a funeral:
a few fistfuls at first,
then shoveled in and
stamped down flat. But
weep not, for in the grave
like stillness, moth shadows
dance across wood slats
to the creak of porch swing
music while iced tea sweats
starshine onto work-worn palms.

Knee Deep in October

And what did I learn, wading
        the river in cool fall evening?
What, after wandering down worn sandstone steps?
        What, while tracing Tishominko's trails?

I learned of sand, sharp with shell and gravel,
        of rocks, smooth and grey and gorgeous,
and I learned the green of fall that drips
        from vines and branches and collects
as algae in pools where caves sprout from under dead logs.

As fresh-fallen dam water pushed each footfall
        further sideways, I wanted it to make meaning,
to be a metaphor for me and my work and the rushing
        of time like leaves on the wind or twigs in the water.

But it was just a river—a creek, actually—and even then
        too wide and winding to mind my wishes.

Mimesis

He is captivated,
captures snapshots
of reflections in
creek water or
polished tile.

There, the world
glosses smooth,
sectionalized. It
cannot expand
forever, framed
by riverbanks
and baseboards
and borders of
pictures taken.
It is controlled,
shows only what is.
No one expects
anything more from it.

It must be nice,
he thinks, to live
in reflections,
where nothing is
quite as definite, and only
the lightest parts
of life happen.

Hello Again, Green

trees of leafy expanse

moss of down
        —laid branch

grass shoots dangling
        from mouth of deer in dead sprint

poison ivy leaf, with oil-burnt
        holes in tri-pattern

youth in summer
        sun splashing

Sprite bottle, bobbing along
        in his wake

snake-doctor, saddling up
        the slithering heel-biter

lichen, expanding
        across stone overlooking

oily film in stagnant pool stocked
        with detritus of living

needles, littering the floor
        beneath straight-armed pine

horse-apple, here,
        miles from any bois d'arc bough

turtle, popping under

soft shell of rippling

water, thick with itself and
        slow, and hiding

fish, whose mouths
        gulp an air fresh and cool like

evening, the first in months the heat of humanity has not overcome
        your balming shade and driven all life indoors to sweat

all the same

Image: Artificial flower in pond, near Durant, OK, 2020

Acknowledgements

Many thanks to the editors, staff, and readers of the following journals and websites which first published the listed poems:

Atlas Poetica 40 (Summer 2020): *Statuary Sequence* ("four-foot flamingo," "concrete children," "stone squirrel," and "angels, saints, the virgin")
The Bamboo Hut, No. 1, 2020 (Jan 2020 online): "Buzzard circles"
Dragon Poet Review (Summer/Fall 2018): "Among the Trees," "Bird Watching," "Raccoon Eyes"
Frogpond 42.2 (Spring/Summer 2019): "a cardinal"
Ninth Letter, Origins (Summer 2019 online): "Revision, June 27"
Red Earth Review, no. 6 (July 2018): "Red Earth Redress" (as "Color Poem")
Red River Review, no. 72 (Aug 2019 online): "Meditation" (as "Meditations: University Green"), and "Visions of Durant, OK"
Tejascovido (April 5, 2020 online): "What I Hope We Remember"
Voices (May 2018): "University Boulevard"

Along with the above, selections from this manuscript have been re-published or accepted for inclusion in the following publications:

"Red Earth Redress" has been republished in **Bull Buffalo and Indian Paintbrush: The Poetry of Oklahoma** (TJMF, 2020), edited by Ron Wallace.

"What I Hope We Remember" has been republished in a special *Tejascovido* edition of **Langdon Review of the Arts in Texas** (Fall 2020).

"Knee Deep in October" is to be included in **Level Land: Poems for and about the I-35 Corridor** (Lamar University Literary Press, 2021), edited by Crag Hill and Todd Fuller.

Photo Credit: Sherri Whisenhunt

Cullen Whisenhunt is a graduate of Oklahoma City University's Red Earth Creative Writing MFA program. He lives and writes in southeastern Oklahoma and has taught English for Southeastern Oklahoma State University in Durant, OK, Murray State College in Tishomingo, OK, and Eastern Oklahoma State College at their McAlester, OK, campus.

www.ingramcontent.com/pod-product-compliance
Lightning Source LLC
Chambersburg PA
CBHW051013050726
47592CB00007B/2833